theirs is the kingdom of heaven

hey shall be comforted. Blessed

herit the earth. Blessed are the

righteousness: for they shall b

they shall obtain mercy. Bles

all see God. Blessed are the pe

he children of God. Blessed ar

hteousness' sake: for theirs is

are you, when men shall revile

l say all manner of evil against

and be exceeding glad: for gr

or so persecuted they the prop

sed are the poor in spirit: for th

But let justice run down like water,
And righteousness like a mighty stream.
Amos 5:24 (NKJV)
— C.B.W.

For Dr. Don Davis, whose heart and thought helped form this book.
— T.L.

Text © 2010 Carole Boston Weatherford
Illustrations © 2010 Tim Ladwig

Published in 2010 by Eerdmans Books for Young Readers
an imprint of Wm. B. Eerdmans Publishing Co.

Wm. B. Eerdmans Publishing Co.
2140 Oak Industrial Dr. NE, Grand Rapids, Michigan 49505
P.O. Box 163, Cambridge CB3 9PU U.K.

www.eerdmans.com/youngreaders

Manufactured at Tien Wah Press in Singapore in April 2010, second printing

10 11 12 13 14 15 16   9 8 7 6 5 4 3 2

Library of Congress Cataloging-in-Publication Data

Weatherford, Carole Boston, 1956-
The Beatitudes : from slavery to civil rights / written by Carole Boston Weatherford ; illustrated by Tim Ladwig.
p. cm.
ISBN 978-0-8028-5352-3 (alk. paper)
1. Civil rights movements — United States — History — Juvenile literature.
2. African Americans — Civil rights — History — Juvenile literature.
3. Racism — United States — History — Juvenile literature.
4. United States — Race relations — History — Juvenile literature.
5. Slavery — United States — History — Juvenile literature.
I. Ladwig, Tim, ill. II. Title.
E185.61.W356 2010
323.0973--dc22

2009026236

The illustrations were rendered in watercolor and pastel on Twinrocker tinted watercolor paper.
The display and text type were set in Adobe Garamond Pro.

THE BEATITUDES

FROM SLAVERY TO CIVIL RIGHTS

Written by Carole Boston Weatherford • Illustrated by Tim Ladwig

Eerdmans Books for Young Readers

Grand Rapids, Michigan • Cambridge, U.K.

BLESSED ARE THE POOR IN SPIRIT:
for theirs is the kingdom of heaven.

BLESSED ARE THEY THAT MOURN:
for they shall be comforted.

BLESSED ARE THE MEEK:
for they shall inherit the earth.

BLESSED ARE THEY WHICH DO HUNGER
AND THIRST AFTER RIGHTEOUSNESS:
for they shall be filled.

BLESSED ARE THE MERCIFUL:
for they shall obtain mercy.

BLESSED ARE THE PURE IN HEART:
for they shall see God.

BLESSED ARE THE PEACEMAKERS:
for they shall be called the children of God.

BLESSED ARE THEY WHICH ARE PERSECUTED
FOR RIGHTEOUSNESS' SAKE:
for theirs is the kingdom of heaven.

BLESSED ARE YOU, when men shall revile you, and persecute you,
and shall say all manner of evil against you falsely, for my sake.

REJOICE, AND BE EXCEEDING GLAD:
for great is your reward in heaven:
for so persecuted they the prophets which were before you.

— Matthew 5:3–12 (KJV)

Since the first African American churches were founded in the 18th century, black religious organizations have brought biblical values to bear on the freedom struggle. Black ministers preached against the institution of slavery, and slaves sang spirituals promising deliverance from bondage. African Americans drew on that same faith during the segregation era. And when the masses rose up against racial oppression during the Civil Rights Movement, they were emboldened by a belief in a just and a compassionate God. They trusted that God was with them and that he would set them free.

Blessed are the poor in spirit: fo

I am the Lord your God.
I was with the Africans who were torn
from the Motherland and cramped in holds of ships
on the Middle Passage from Africa to the Americas.
I heard them chant: *Kum ba ya, kum ba ya.*

theirs is the kingdom of heaven

Blessed are they that mourn: fo

R Allen

Absalom Jones

James Varick

I was with Richard Allen, Absalom Jones, and James Varick,
who founded churches where African Americans
could praise the Lord and shout "Hallelujah!"
I rang the church bells.

hey shall be comforted. Blesse

d are the meek: for they shall i

I was with Harriet Tubman when she fled slavery.
As she led others out of bondage,
I was the star guiding them north.

which do hunger and thirst aft

I was with the U.S. Colored Troops
who fought to end slavery during the Civil War.
I beat the drum for freedom.

filled. Blessed are the merciful

I was with Booker T. Washington
and Mary McLeod Bethune, who built colleges
and lit the way for young minds.
I was the lamp.

re the pure in heart: for they

I was with Marian Anderson when she sang spirituals
on the steps of the Lincoln Memorial
after the Daughters of the American Revolution
barred her from performing in their concert hall.
I was the microphone.

I was with Rosa Parks when she was arrested
for refusing to give up her seat to a white man
on a Montgomery city bus.
And I was with the citizens who walked
rather than ride buses during the boycott.
I was their shoes.

nakers: for they shall be called

he children of God. Blessed a

EMMETT TILL

I was with the mother
of fourteen-year-old lynching victim Emmett Till.
As she stood at his casket, sobbing,
I was the shoulder she leaned on.

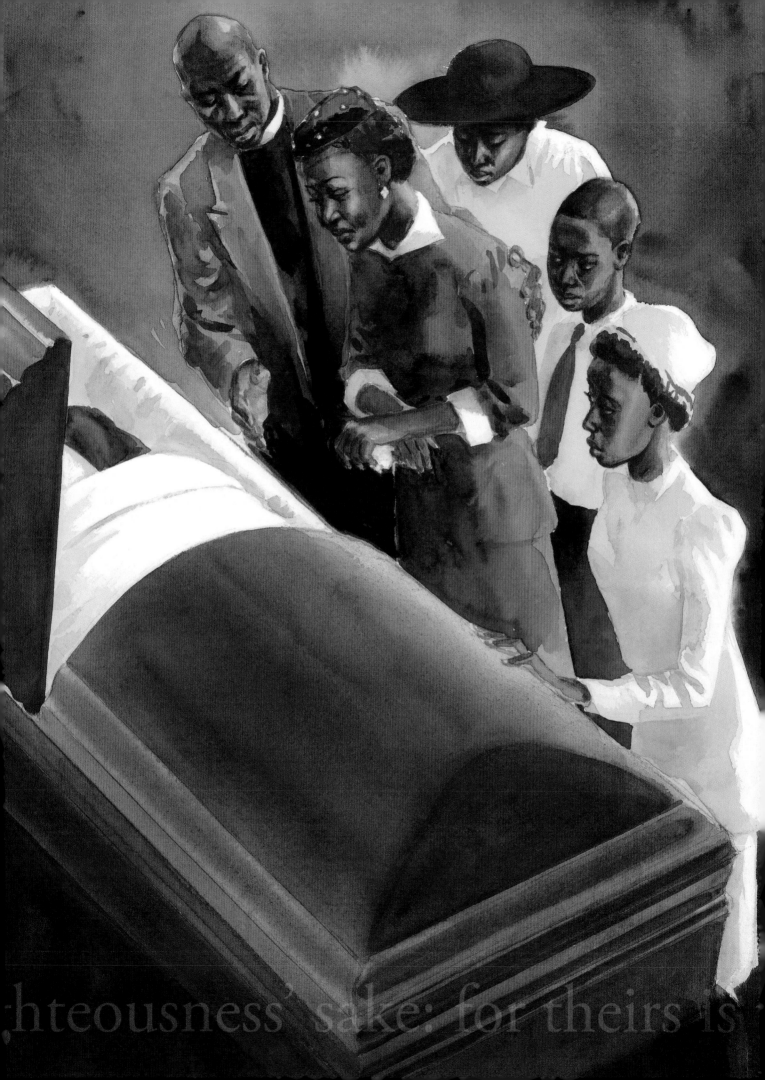

hteousness' sake: for theirs is

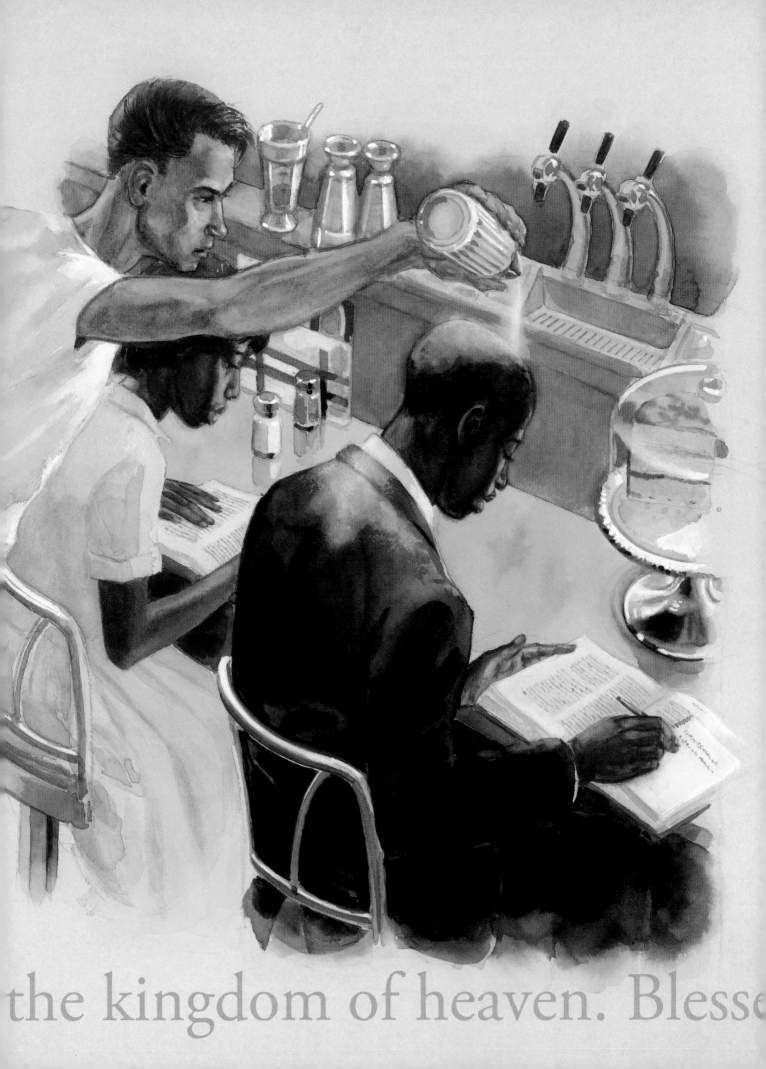

the kingdom of heaven. Blesse

I was on the Freedom Rides
and at the lunch counter sit-ins.
I sat alongside the protesters.

are you, when men shall revil

I was with Martin Luther King Jr. when he shared his dream
of brotherhood at the March on Washington.
And when peaceful protesters in the Selma to Montgomery march
were beaten by police on an Alabama bridge,
I nursed the wounded.

you, and persecute you, and s

I say all manner of evil agains

I was with six-year-old Ruby Bridges
when angry whites heckled her as she entered
an all-white elementary school to become its first black student.
I held her hand.

great is your reward in heaven

I was with Mississippi political organizer Fannie Lou Hamer
when she got sick and tired of being sick and tired
and demanded the right to vote.
When she breathed song into the struggle,
I shook the tambourine.

I was with Barack Obama
when he took his oath
as President of the United States.
I was the Bible where he placed his hand.

Blessed are the poor in spirit:

for theirs is the kingdom of hea

I was with your ancestors and I will be with your offspring,
standing on the side of justice.
Even now, I am with the downtrodden
and with those who seek uplift.
I am holy water in the stream of humanity.
Drink, bathe, and be free.

en. Blessed are they that mourn

RICHARD ALLEN (1760–1831)
Born a slave in Philadelphia, Allen started preaching and bought his freedom at age seventeen. He and fellow preacher Absalom Jones walked out of services at a white church in 1787 after black worshipers were forced to sit in the balcony. After cofounding the Free African Society and The African Church, Allen went on to establish Bethel African Methodist Church (now known as Mother Bethel A.M.E. Church) in Philadelphia. In 1816 Allen organized the African Methodist Episcopal Church, the first black denomination.

MARIAN ANDERSON (1897–1993)
Born in Philadelphia, Anderson sang so well in the church choir that her church and community paid for her to take voice lessons. By 1917 she was performing solo concerts. She was renowned in Europe and in 1955 became the first African American to sing at New York's Metropolitan Opera House. Her most historic concert took place on Easter Sunday, 1939, on the steps of the Lincoln Memorial after she was barred from performing at Constitution Hall due to the color of her skin.

MARY McLEOD BETHUNE (1875–1955)
Born in a cabin in Mayesville, South Carolina, Bethune was sponsored to a mission school and won a scholarship to Moody Bible Institute in Chicago before founding the Daytona Normal and Industrial School for Negro Girls in Daytona Beach, Florida. Early on, she ran the school on little more than faith, once having her students bake sweet potato pies to help fund expansion. The institution is now known as Bethune-Cookman College. She advised several presidents and was one of the most influential African American women of her time. Bethune's Last Will and Testament contained nine values — including faith, hope, and love — that she left for future generations.

RUBY BRIDGES (1954–)
Born in Mississippi, Bridges became, at age six, the first African American student to integrate the all-white William Frantz Public School in New Orleans. Facing angry crowds on her way to school in 1960, she prayed — just as her mother told her — to fight off fear. Her bravery inspired Norman Rockwell's 1964 painting *The Problem We All Live With*.

FANNIE LOU HAMER (1917–1977)
Born to a Mississippi sharecropping family, Hamer was the twentieth of twenty children. She became determined after a 1962 Civil Rights rally to register herself and others to vote. In her effort, she was severely beaten twice, jailed, and thrown off the plantation. Sustained by faith, she traveled the country pushing for voting rights and sometimes sang spirituals at rallies. In 1964 she founded the Mississippi Freedom Party. On her tombstone are the words "I am sick and tired of being sick and tired."

ABSALOM JONES (1746–1818)
Born a slave in Delaware, Jones bought his own and his family's freedom, became a lay preacher for blacks, and, with Richard Allen, walked out of a white church that ordered blacks to the balcony. Jones, Allen, and others formed the Free African Society, and in 1791 organized The African Church that became the African Episcopal Church of St. Thomas, the first black Episcopal parish in the U.S. In 1804 Jones was ordained a priest, the nation's first Episcopal priest of African descent.

MARTIN LUTHER KING JR. (1929–1968)
Born in Atlanta, King followed his father into the Baptist ministry and became a leader of the Civil Rights Movement. An advocate of nonviolence, he led the Montgomery Bus Boycott and the March from Selma to Montgomery. He wrote the spiritually moving

"Letter from Birmingham Jail," delivered the "I Have a Dream" speech at the 1963 March on Washington, and preached his "I've Been to the Mountaintop" sermon on the night before his assassination.

BARACK OBAMA (1961–)

Born in Honolulu, Hawaii, to a Kansas-born mother and a Kenyan father, Obama graduated from Columbia University and Harvard Law School, where he was the first black president of the prestigious *Harvard Law Review*. After working as a community organizer, a civil rights lawyer, and a law professor, he was elected to the Illinois State Senate. He won a U.S. Senate seat in 2004 and was elected the 44th President of the United States in 2008 — the first African American to hold that office.

ROSA PARKS (1913–2005)

Born in Tuskegee, Alabama, Parks worked quietly with the National Association for the Advancement of Colored People (NAACP) to gain equal rights for African Americans. She was employed as a seamstress when her 1955 arrest for refusing to give up her seat on a city bus to a white passenger sparked the Montgomery Bus Boycott. The boycott was led by Martin Luther King Jr., who was then a young minister.

EMMETT TILL (1941–1955)

While visiting his uncle in Mississippi, Chicago teen Emmett Till took a dare and flirted with a white store clerk. He was kidnapped, lynched, and thrown in the Tallahatchie River. When his disfigured body was recovered, his mother had an open-casket funeral, so the world would know what happened to her son.

HARRIET TUBMAN (c. 1820–1913)

Born a slave on the Eastern Shore of Maryland, Harriet Tubman fled to Philadelphia in 1849. Communing with God as friend to friend, she heeded his call to become a conductor, a guide, on the Underground Railroad. Strengthened by faith, she risked her own life to lead her family and countless others to freedom.

JAMES VARICK (1750–1827)

Born a slave near Newburgh, New York, Varick, a shoemaker by trade, became a Methodist preacher and in 1796 left the church that licensed him in order to form the African Methodist Episcopal Zion Church. Dedicated in 1800, it was New York's first African American church. Varick often preached against slavery and injustice and was a cofounder of *Freedom's Journal*, the nation's first African American newspaper. In 1822 he became the first bishop of the A.M.E. Zion Church.

BOOKER T. WASHINGTON (1856–1915)

Born a slave in Virginia, Booker T. Washington was an educator, orator, and advocate of self-improvement. He thought that hard work, individual responsibility, and a strong moral and spiritual fiber were crucial to achieving racial equality. In 1881 he became the first principal of Tuskegee Institute in Alabama, which equipped blacks for jobs in education, agriculture, and trades. The school is now known as Tuskegee University.

Blessed are the poor in spirit: fo
lessed are they that mourn: for
d are the meek: for they shall i
which do hunger and thirst aft
illed. Blessed are the merciful:
re the pure in heart: for they s
makers: for they shall be called
hey which are persecuted for i
he kingdom of heaven. Blesse
you, and persecute you, and sh
you falsely, for my sake. Rejoic
great is your reward in heaven:
hets which were before you. B